Austin Huang
黄晓枫

Piano Concerto "2020"

April 24, 2020
Seattle, Washington
USA
美国西雅图

Sound Press
Bellevue, Washington
USA

Orchestra

1 Piccolo
2 Flutes
2 Oboes
2 Clarinets in B♭
2 Bassoons

4 Horns in F
3 Trumpets in B♭
2 Trombones
1 Bass Trombone
1 Tuba

Timpani
Cymbals

Solo Piano

Violin 1
Violin 2
Viola
Celli
Bass

During the 2020 Covid-19 global pandemic, I composed this exciting piece while staying home ordered by the Washington State Governor in April 2020. The music was composed to explore a new idea for classical music with inclusion of contemporary music generated from contemporary composing technologies. Thus, the music consists both classical passages and contemporary sections in the music development. It brings beautiful classical style flowing melody to listeners as walking in a scene of beautiful nature blooming and also pushes listeners up to the apex of snow cap of Himalaya. The listening experience is fresh with both classical beauty and high strength of tension stimulating listeners' nerve.

在中国人的记忆里庚子年是刻入骨髓的灾难之年。2020年又是庚子年。大年二十九（1月23日）武汉封城，新冠病毒肆虐。而后，新冠病毒相继攻破了中东、欧洲、美国、和澳洲，第三次世界大战就此开打病毒与人类的战争。

武汉封城期间，看到那么多的令人感动的事迹。来自全国的医护人员支援武汉，年轻的女护士剃光头宣誓，令我无比感动。中国正是由于有这么多的仁人志士，每在关键时刻挺身而出，才使得中华民族绵延不绝。

疫情期间,所有的活动都停摆了。居家防疫，也没有其它活动了，有了整块的时间。于是就一鼓作气创作了这部钢琴协奏曲《2020》。耗时二周多，从4月8日至4月23日。当然，之前13年的创作体会，加上最近几年应对音乐巡讲的需要，对之前创作的作品进行了分析，尤其对理论方面的深度探索和思考，形成了自己的想法。这部作品就是应用自己形成的想法，尝试中西结合和古典与现代结合的一次具体探索实践的努力。

Austin Huang 黄晓枫
2020.4.25
Bellevue Washington, USA
于西雅图

Piano Concerto "2020"
钢琴协奏曲《2020》

Austin Huang
黄晓枫
April 24, 2020
Seattle 西雅图

9
♩=120
Picc.
Fl. 1
Fl. 2
Ob. 1
Ob. 2
Cl. 1
Cl. 2
Bsn. 1
Bsn. 2
Hn. 1
Hn. 2
Hn. 3
Hn. 4
Tpt.1
Tpt. 2
Tpt. 3
Tbn. 1
Tbn. 2
B. Tbn.
Tba.
Timp.
Cym.
Pno.
fff
p
mp
Ped.
♩=120
Vln. I
Vln. II
Vla.
div.
Vc.
Db.

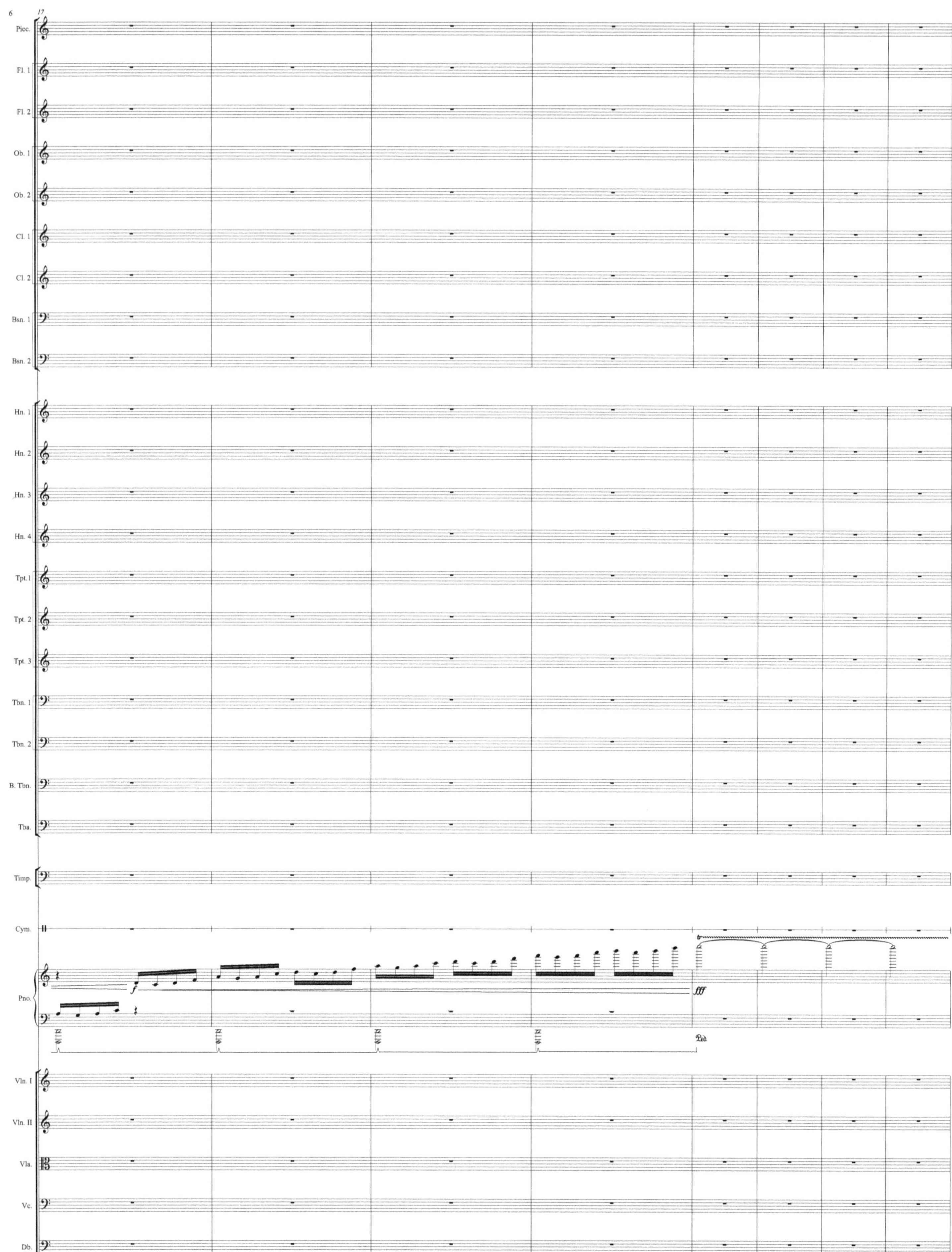
17
Picc.
Fl. 1
Fl. 2
Ob. 1
Ob. 2
Cl. 1
Cl. 2
Bsn. 1
Bsn. 2
Hn. 1
Hn. 2
Hn. 3
Hn. 4
Tpt. 1
Tpt. 2
Tpt. 3
Tbn. 1
Tbn. 2
B. Tbn.
Tba.
Timp.
Cym.
Pno.
f
fff
Ped.
Vln. I
Vln. II
Vla.
Vc.
Db.

25
Picc.
Fl. 1
Fl. 2
Ob. 1
Ob. 2
Cl. 1
Cl. 2
Bsn. 1
Bsn. 2
Hn. 1
Hn. 2
Hn. 3
Hn. 4
Tpt. 1
Tpt. 2
Tpt. 3
Tbn. 1
Tbn. 2
B. Tbn.
Tba.
Timp.
Cym.
Pno.
Vln. I
Vln. II
Vla.
Vc.
Db.
=140
unis.

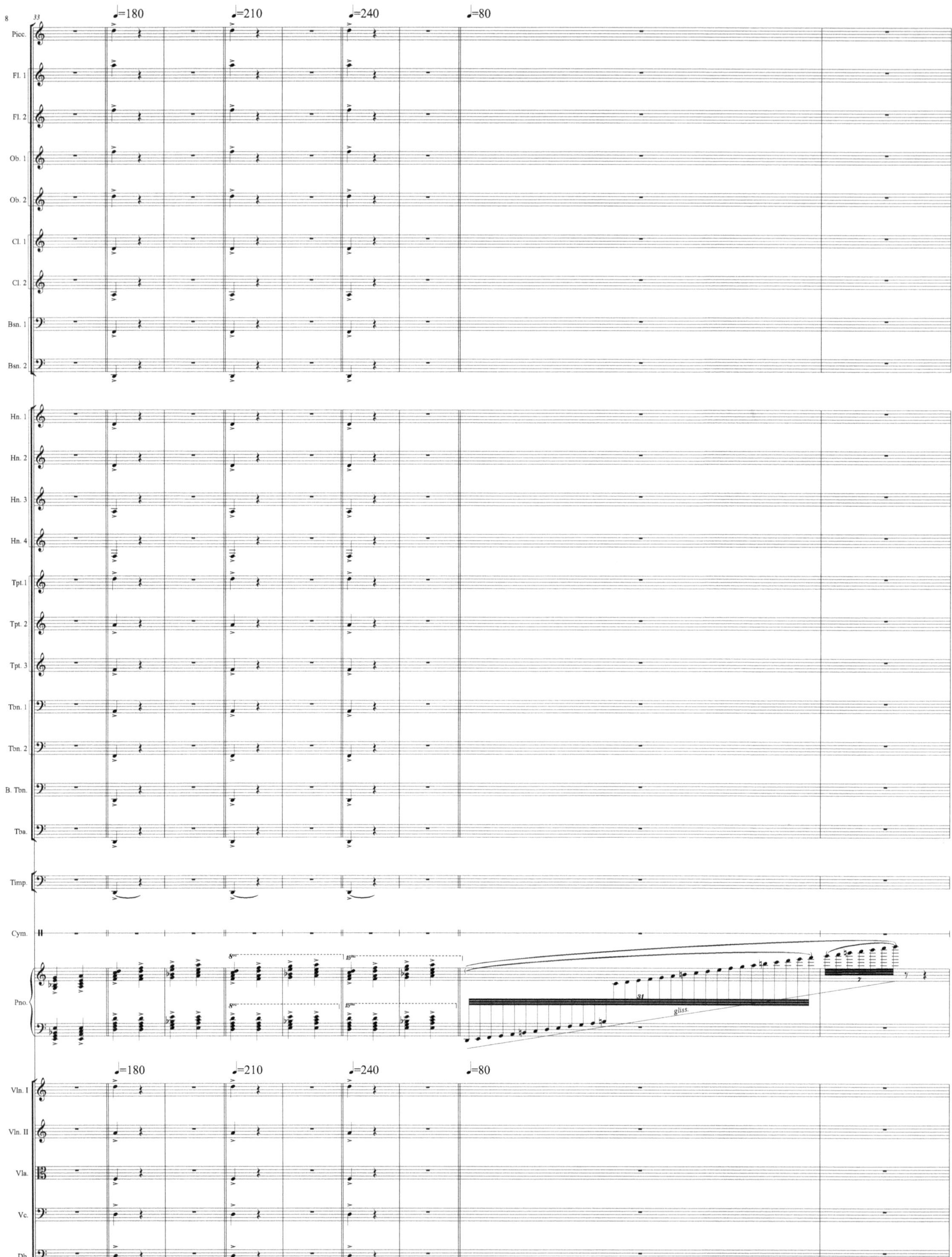
33
♩=180
♩=210
♩=240
♩=80
Picc.
Fl. 1
Fl. 2
Ob. 1
Ob. 2
Cl. 1
Cl. 2
Bsn. 1
Bsn. 2
Hn. 1
Hn. 2
Hn. 3
Hn. 4
Tpt. 1
Tpt. 2
Tpt. 3
Tbn. 1
Tbn. 2
B. Tbn.
Tba.
Timp.
Cym.
Pno.
gliss.
Vln. I
Vln. II
Vla.
Vc.
Db.

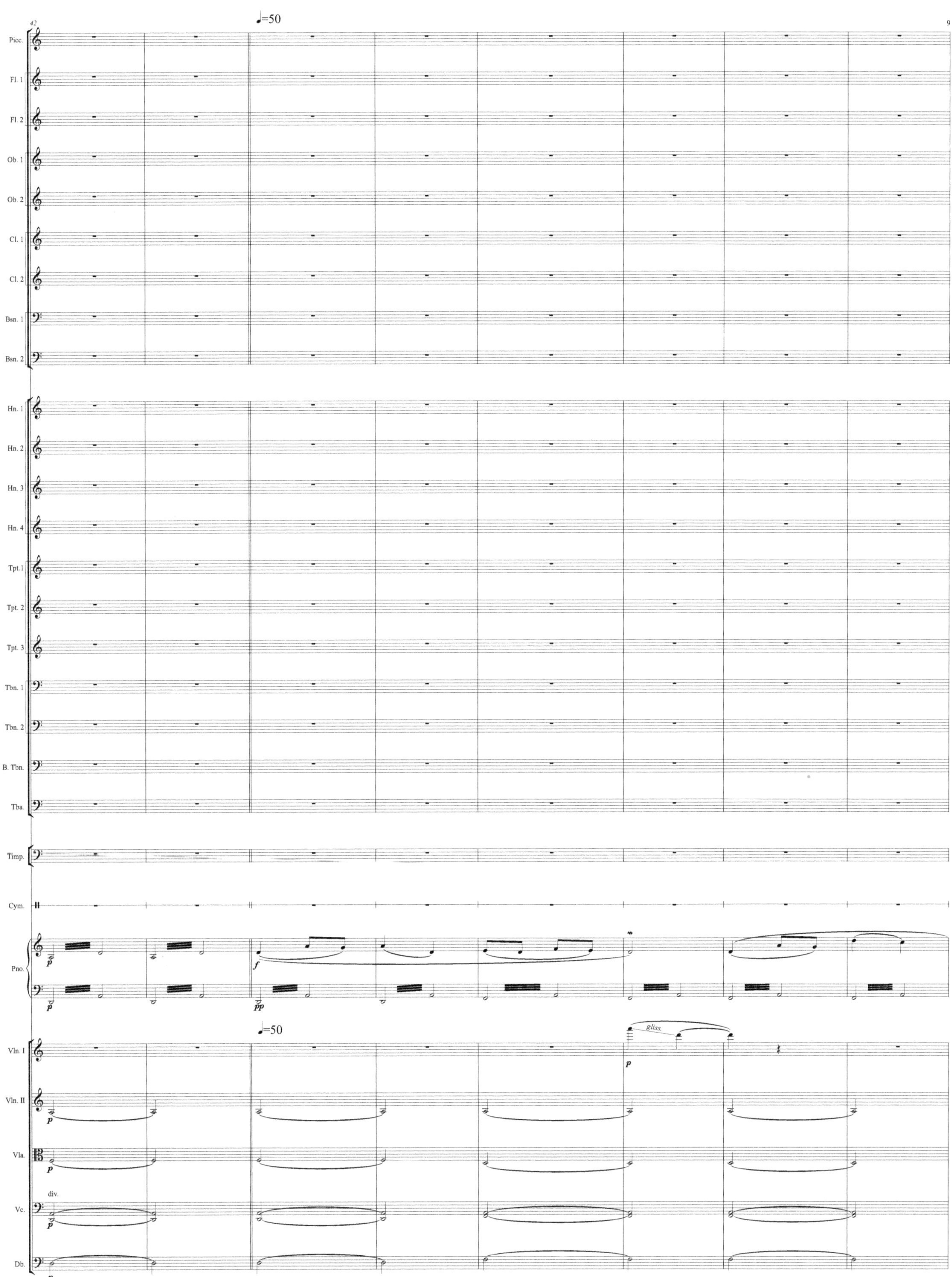
42
♩=50
Picc.
Fl. 1
Fl. 2
Ob. 1
Ob. 2
Cl. 1
Cl. 2
Bsn. 1
Bsn. 2
Hn. 1
Hn. 2
Hn. 3
Hn. 4
Tpt. 1
Tpt. 2
Tpt. 3
Tbn. 1
Tbn. 2
B. Tbn.
Tba.
Timp.
Cym.
Pno.
p
f
pp
♩=50
gliss.
Vln. I
Vln. II
Vla.
div.
Vc.
Db.

50
Picc.
Fl. 1
Fl. 2
Ob. 1
Ob. 2
Cl. 1
Cl. 2
Bsn. 1
Bsn. 2
Hn. 1
Hn. 2
Hn. 3
Hn. 4
Tpt.1
Tpt. 2
Tpt. 3
Tbn. 1
Tbn. 2
B. Tbn.
Tba.
Timp.
Cym.
Pno.
gliss.
gliss.
Vln. I
Vln. II
Vla.
Vc.
Db.

58
Picc.
Fl. 1
Fl. 2
Ob. 1
Ob. 2
Cl. 1
Cl. 2
Bsn. 1
Bsn. 2
Hn. 1
Hn. 2
Hn. 3
Hn. 4
Tpt. 1
Tpt. 2
Tpt. 3
Tbn. 1
Tbn. 2
B. Tbn.
Tba.
Timp.
Cym.
Pno.
Vln. I
Vln. II
Vla.
Vc.
Db.
gliss.
mf
mp
unis.
div.

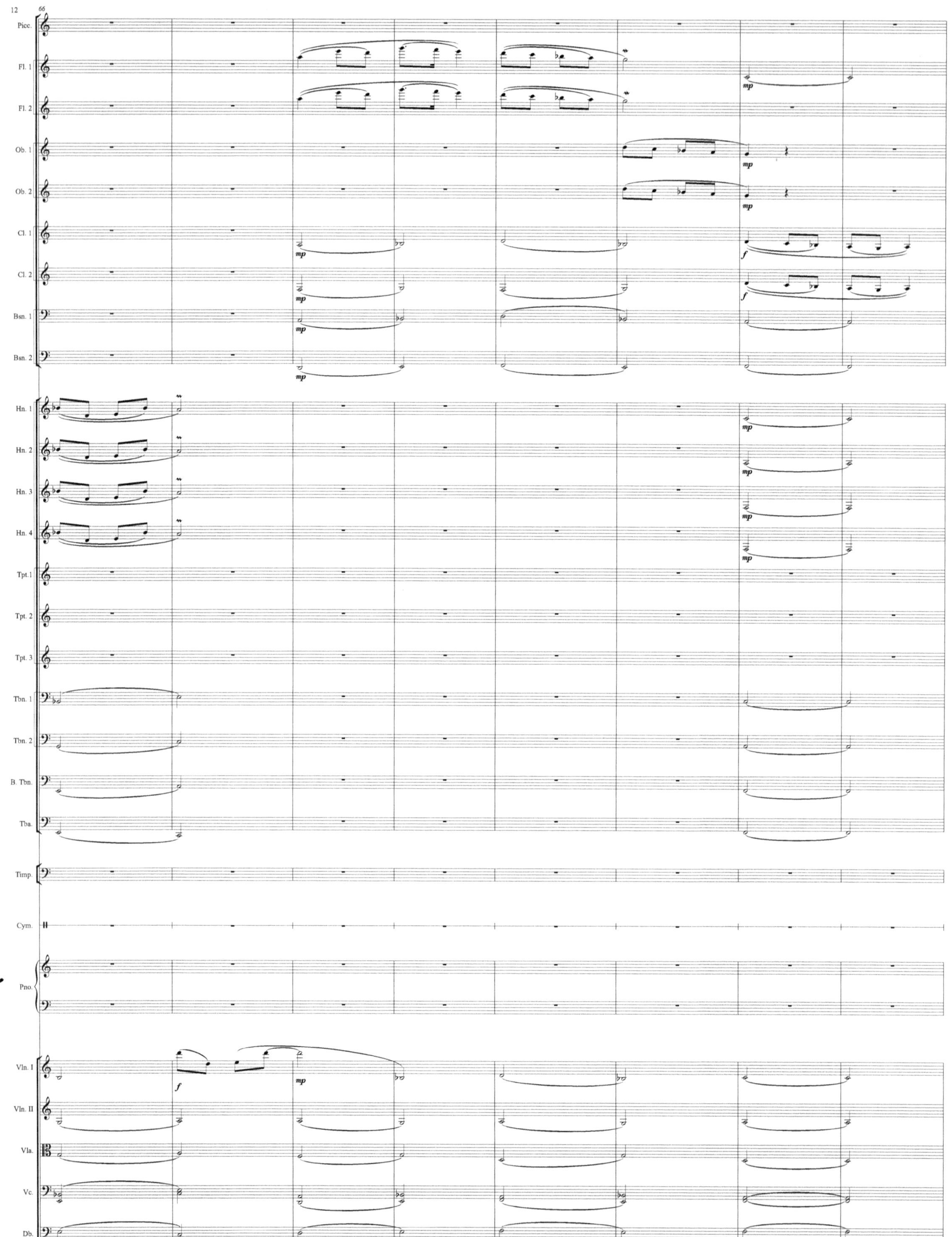
66
Picc.
Fl. 1
Fl. 2
Ob. 1
Ob. 2
Cl. 1
Cl. 2
Bsn. 1
Bsn. 2
Hn. 1
Hn. 2
Hn. 3
Hn. 4
Tpt. 1
Tpt. 2
Tpt. 3
Tbn. 1
Tbn. 2
B. Tbn.
Tba.
Timp.
Cym.
Pno.
Vln. I
Vln. II
Vla.
Vc.
Db.
mp
f

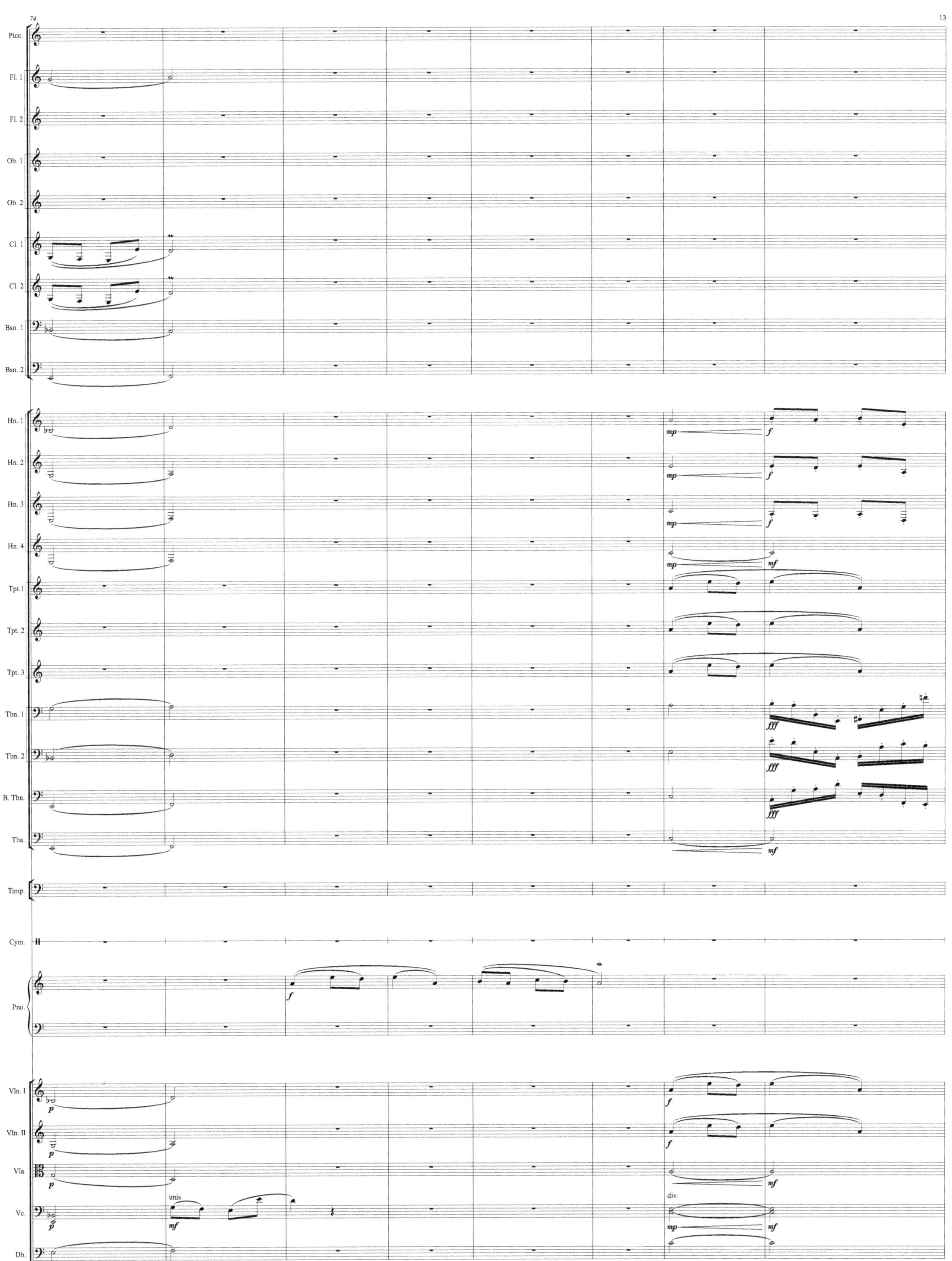
74
Picc.
Fl. 1
Fl. 2
Ob. 1
Ob. 2
Cl. 1
Cl. 2
Bsn. 1
Bsn. 2
Hn. 1
Hn. 2
Hn. 3
Hn. 4
Tpt. 1
Tpt. 2
Tpt. 3
Tbn. 1
Tbn. 2
B. Tbn.
Tba.
Timp.
Cym.
Pno.
Vln. I
Vln. II
Vla.
Vc.
Db.
mp
f
mf
fff
p
unis.
div.

82
Picc.
Fl. 1
Fl. 2
Ob. 1
Ob. 2
Cl. 1
Cl. 2
Bsn. 1
Bsn. 2
Hn. 1
Hn. 2
Hn. 3
Hn. 4
Tpt. 1
Tpt. 2
Tpt. 3
Tbn. 1
Tbn. 2
B. Tbn.
Tba.
Timp.
Cym.
Pno.
Vln. I
Vln. II
Vla.
Vc.
Db.
19
22

90
Picc.
Fl. 1
Fl. 2
Ob. 1
Ob. 2
Cl. 1
Cl. 2
Bsn. 1
Bsn. 2
Hn. 1
Hn. 2
Hn. 3
Hn. 4
Tpt. 1
Tpt. 2
Tpt. 3
Tbn. 1
Tbn. 2
B. Tbn.
Tba.
Timp.
Cym.
Pno.
Vln. I
Vln. II
Vla.
Vc.
Db.

98
Picc.
Fl. 1
Fl. 2
Ob. 1
Ob. 2
Cl. 1
Cl. 2
Bsn. 1
Bsn. 2
Hn. 1
Hn. 2
Hn. 3
Hn. 4
Tpt.1
Tpt. 2
Tpt. 3
Tbn. 1
Tbn. 2
B. Tbn.
Tba.
Timp.
Cym.
Pno.
Vln. I
Vln. II
Vla.
Vc.
Db.
mp

106
Picc.
Fl. 1
Fl. 2
Ob. 1
Ob. 2
Cl. 1
Cl. 2
Bsn. 1
Bsn. 2
Hn. 1
Hn. 2
Hn. 3
Hn. 4
Tpt. 1
Tpt. 2
Tpt. 3
Tbn. 1
Tbn. 2
B. Tbn.
Tba.
Timp.
Cym.
Pno.
Vln. I
Vln. II
Vla.
Vc.
Db.

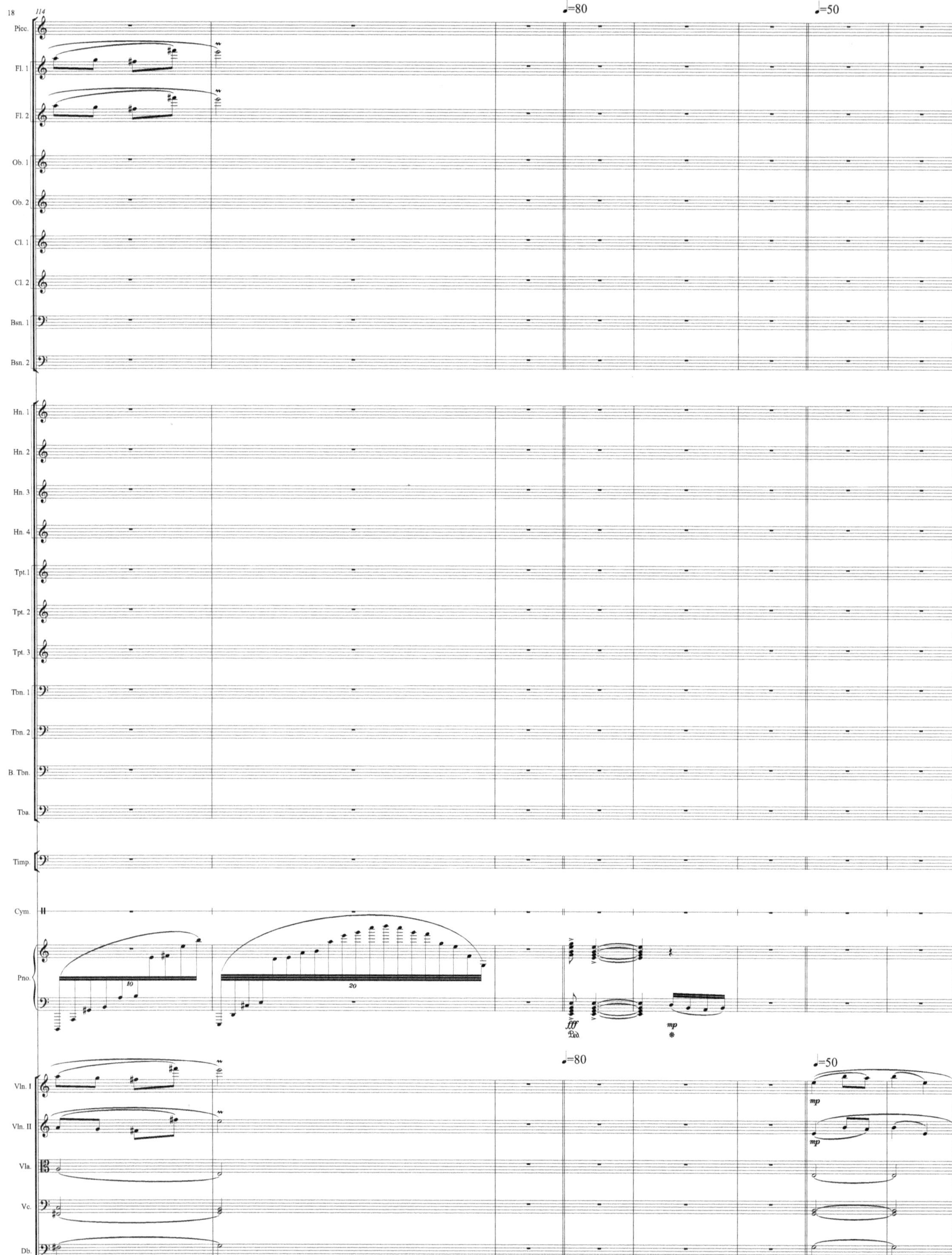
114
♩=80
♩=50
Picc.
Fl. 1
Fl. 2
Ob. 1
Ob. 2
Cl. 1
Cl. 2
Bsn. 1
Bsn. 2
Hn. 1
Hn. 2
Hn. 3
Hn. 4
Tpt.1
Tpt. 2
Tpt. 3
Tbn. 1
Tbn. 2
B. Tbn.
Tba.
Timp.
Cym.
Pno.
10
20
fff
mp
Vln. I
Vln. II
Vla.
Vc.
Db.

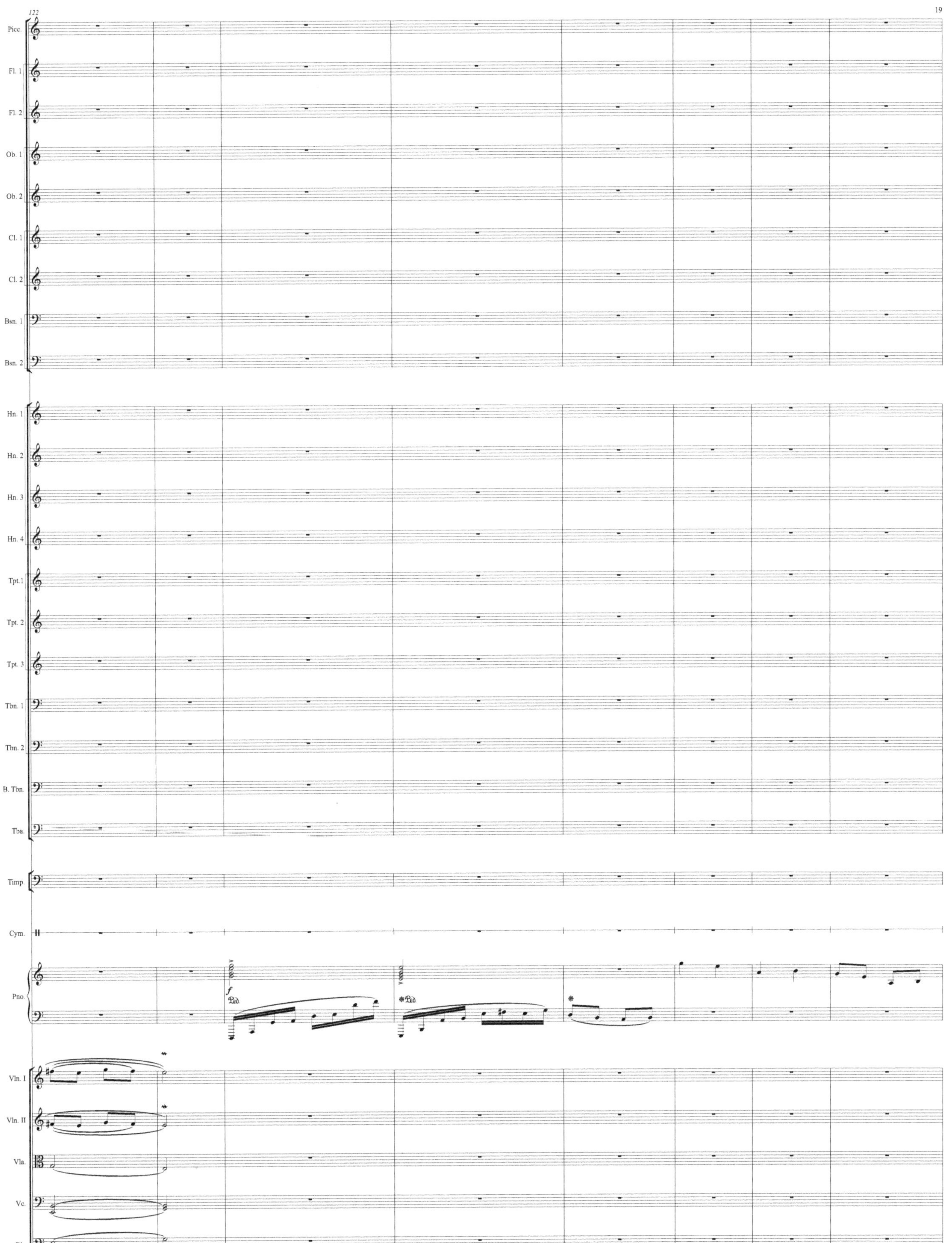
122
Picc.
Fl. 1
Fl. 2
Ob. 1
Ob. 2
Cl. 1
Cl. 2
Bsn. 1
Bsn. 2
Hn. 1
Hn. 2
Hn. 3
Hn. 4
Tpt. 1
Tpt. 2
Tpt. 3
Tbn. 1
Tbn. 2
B. Tbn.
Tba.
Timp.
Cym.
Pno.
f
Ped.
Vln. I
Vln. II
Vla.
Vc.
Db.

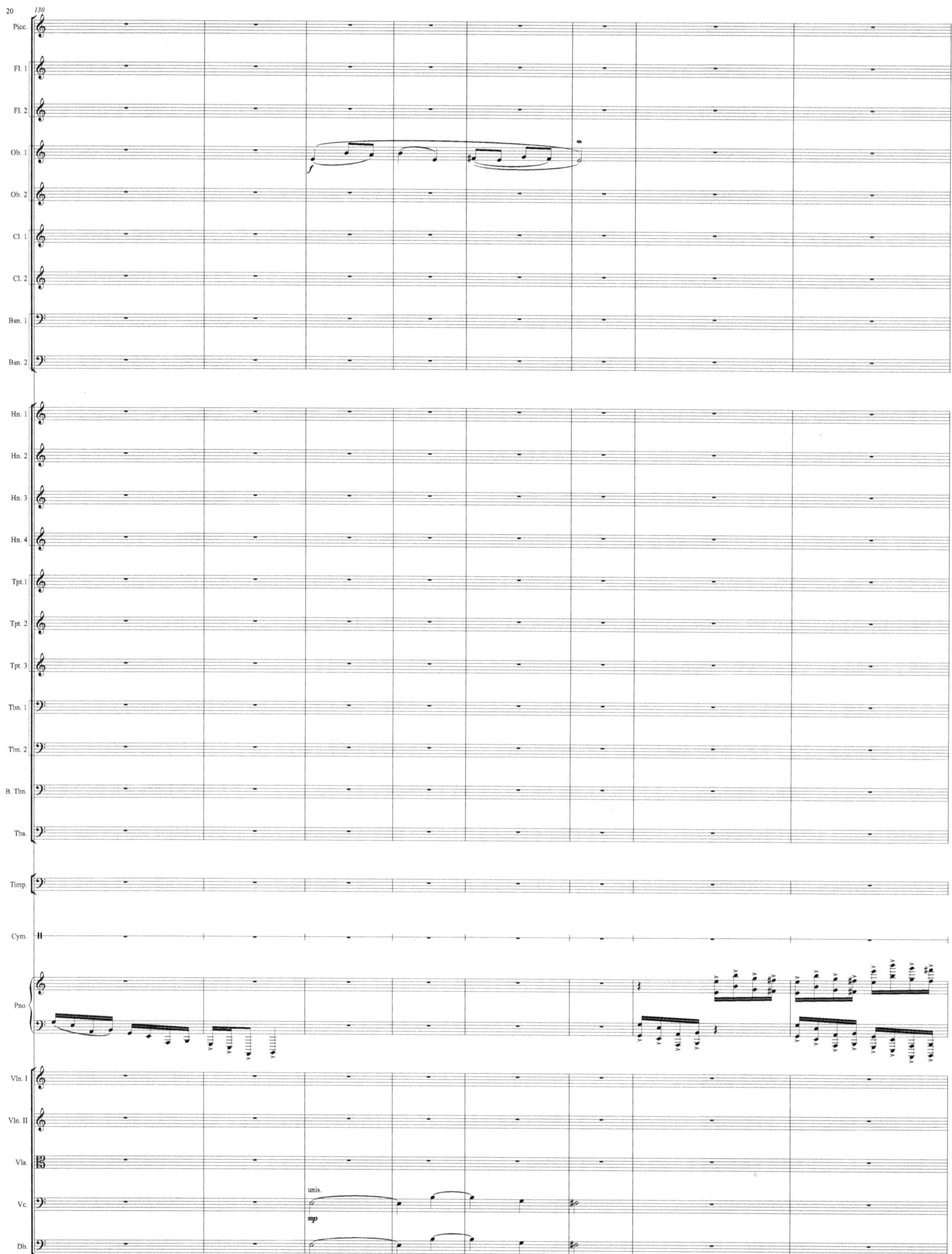
130
Picc.
Fl. 1
Fl. 2
Ob. 1
f
Ob. 2
Cl. 1
Cl. 2
Bsn. 1
Bsn. 2
Hn. 1
Hn. 2
Hn. 3
Hn. 4
Tpt. 1
Tpt. 2
Tpt. 3
Tbn. 1
Tbn. 2
B. Tbn.
Tba.
Timp.
Cym.
Pno.
Vln. I
Vln. II
Vla.
unis.
Vc.
mp
Db.
mp

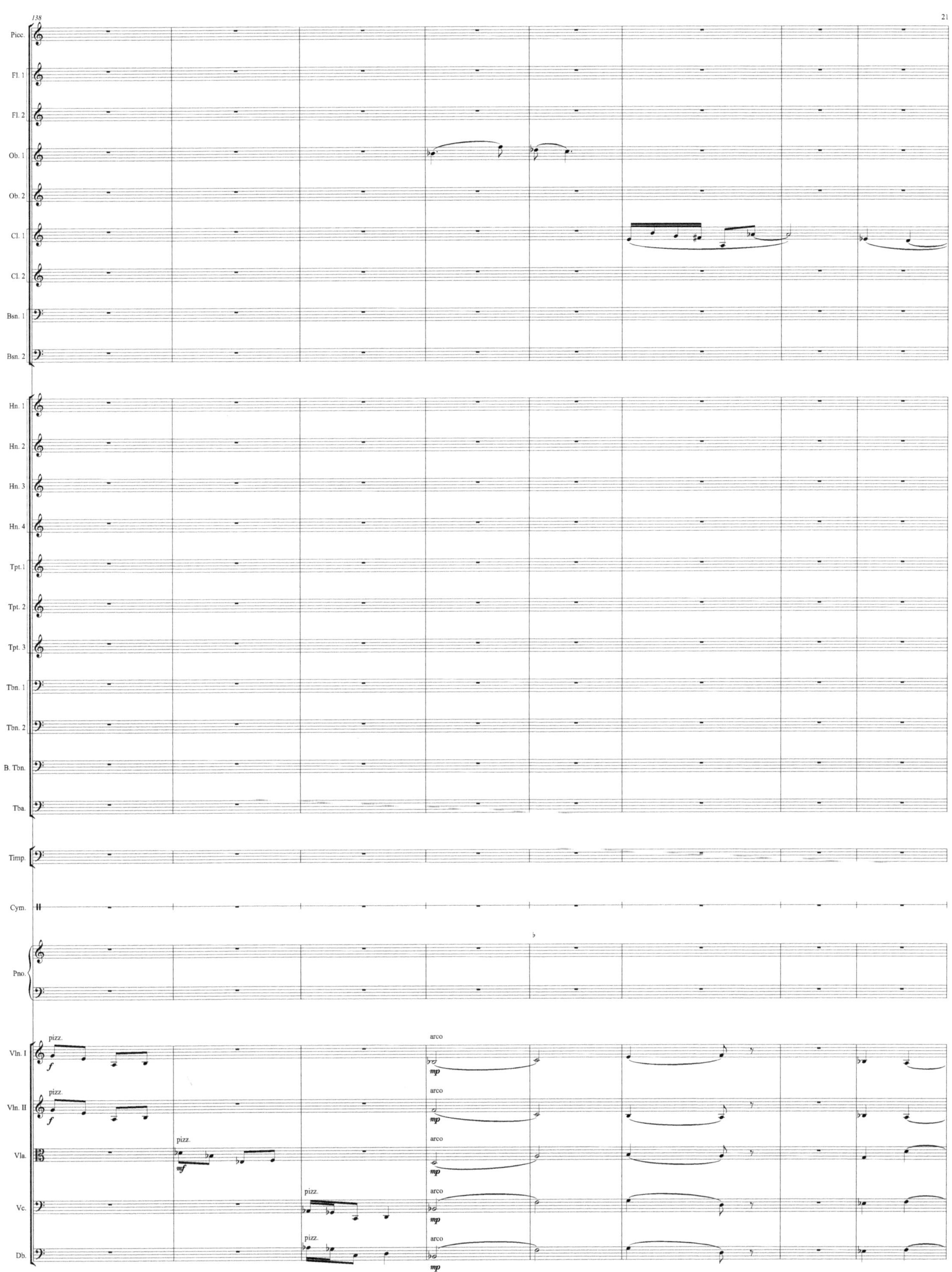
138
Picc.
Fl. 1
Fl. 2
Ob. 1
Ob. 2
Cl. 1
Cl. 2
Bsn. 1
Bsn. 2
Hn. 1
Hn. 2
Hn. 3
Hn. 4
Tpt. 1
Tpt. 2
Tpt. 3
Tbn. 1
Tbn. 2
B. Tbn.
Tba.
Timp.
Cym.
Pno.
Vln. I
pizz.
f
arco
mp
Vln. II
pizz.
f
arco
mp
Vla.
pizz.
mf
arco
mp
Vc.
pizz.
arco
mp
Db.
pizz.
arco
mp

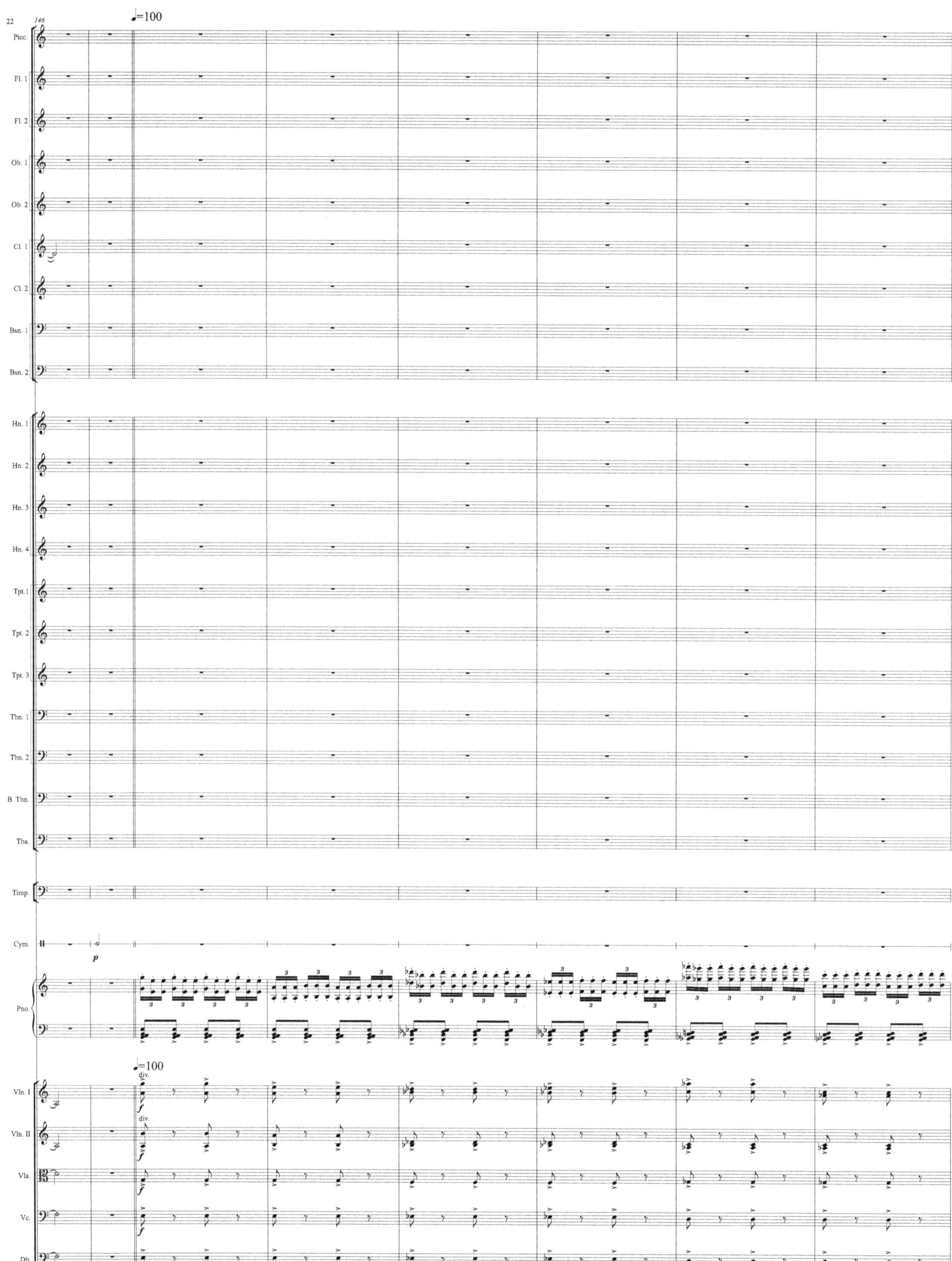
146
♩=100
Picc.
Fl. 1
Fl. 2
Ob. 1
Ob. 2
Cl. 1
Cl. 2
Bsn. 1
Bsn. 2
Hn. 1
Hn. 2
Hn. 3
Hn. 4
Tpt. 1
Tpt. 2
Tpt. 3
Tbn. 1
Tbn. 2
B. Tbn.
Tba.
Timp.
Cym.
p
Pno.
♩=100
div.
Vln. I
f
div.
Vln. II
f
Vla.
f
Vc.
f
Db.
f

154
Picc.
Fl. 1
Fl. 2
Ob. 1
Ob. 2
Cl. 1
Cl. 2
Bsn. 1
Bsn. 2
Hn. 1
Hn. 2
Hn. 3
Hn. 4
Tpt. 1
Tpt. 2
Tpt. 3
Tbn. 1
Tbn. 2
B. Tbn.
Tba.
Timp.
Cym.
Pno.
Vln. I
Vln. II
Vla.
Vc.
Db.
gliss.

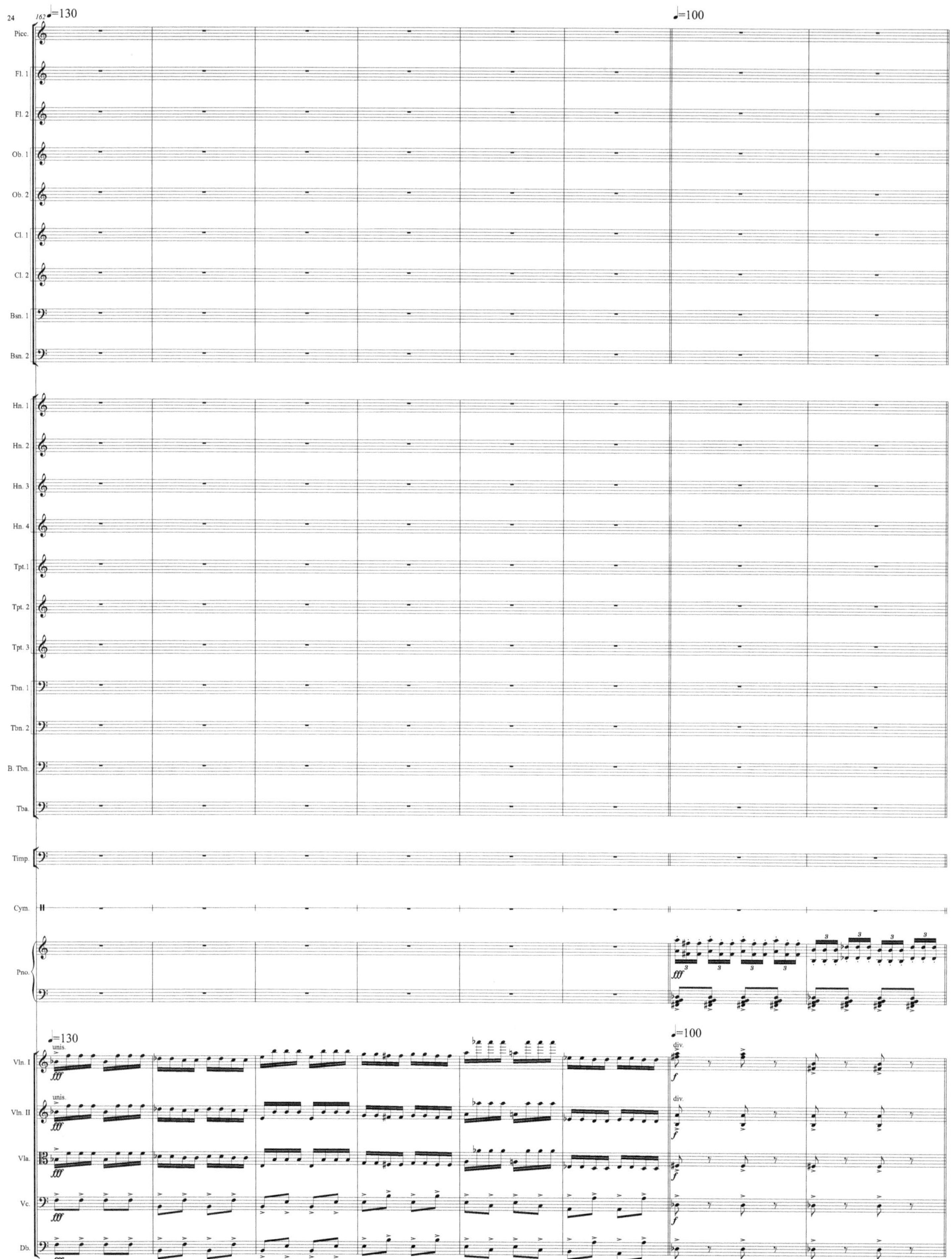
162
♩=130
♩=100
Picc.
Fl. 1
Fl. 2
Ob. 1
Ob. 2
Cl. 1
Cl. 2
Bsn. 1
Bsn. 2
Hn. 1
Hn. 2
Hn. 3
Hn. 4
Tpt. 1
Tpt. 2
Tpt. 3
Tbn. 1
Tbn. 2
B. Tbn.
Tba.
Timp.
Cym.
Pno.
unis.
div.
Vln. I
Vln. II
Vla.
Vc.
Db.

170

♩=130 ♩=100 ♩=130 ♩=100

Picc.
Fl. 1
Fl. 2
Ob. 1
Ob. 2
Cl. 1
Cl. 2
Bsn. 1
Bsn. 2
Hn. 1
Hn. 2
Hn. 3
Hn. 4
Tpt. 1
Tpt. 2
Tpt. 3
Tbn. 1
Tbn. 2
B. Tbn.
Tba.
Timp.
Cym.
Pno.

♩=130 unis. fff ♩=100 div. f ♩=130 unis. fff ♩=100 div. f

Vln. I
Vln. II
Vla.
Vc.
Db.

♩=130
♩=100
178
Picc.
Fl. 1
Fl. 2
Ob. 1
Ob. 2
Cl. 1
Cl. 2
Bsn. 1
Bsn. 2
Hn. 1
Hn. 2
Hn. 3
Hn. 4
Tpt. 1
Tpt. 2
Tpt. 3
Tbn. 1
Tbn. 2
B. Tbn.
Tba.
Timp.
Cym.
Pno.
gliss.
unis.
div.
Vln. I
Vln. II
Vla.
Vc.
Db.

186
♩=50
Picc.
Fl. 1
Fl. 2
Ob. 1
Ob. 2
Cl. 1
Cl. 2
Bsn. 1
Bsn. 2
Hn. 1
Hn. 2
Hn. 3
Hn. 4
Tpt.1
Tpt. 2
Tpt. 3
Tbn. 1
gliss.
f
fff
Tbn. 2
B. Tbn.
Tba.
Timp.
Cym.
Pno.
3
♩=50
unis.
Vln. I
mp
Vln. II
Vla.
Vc.
Db.

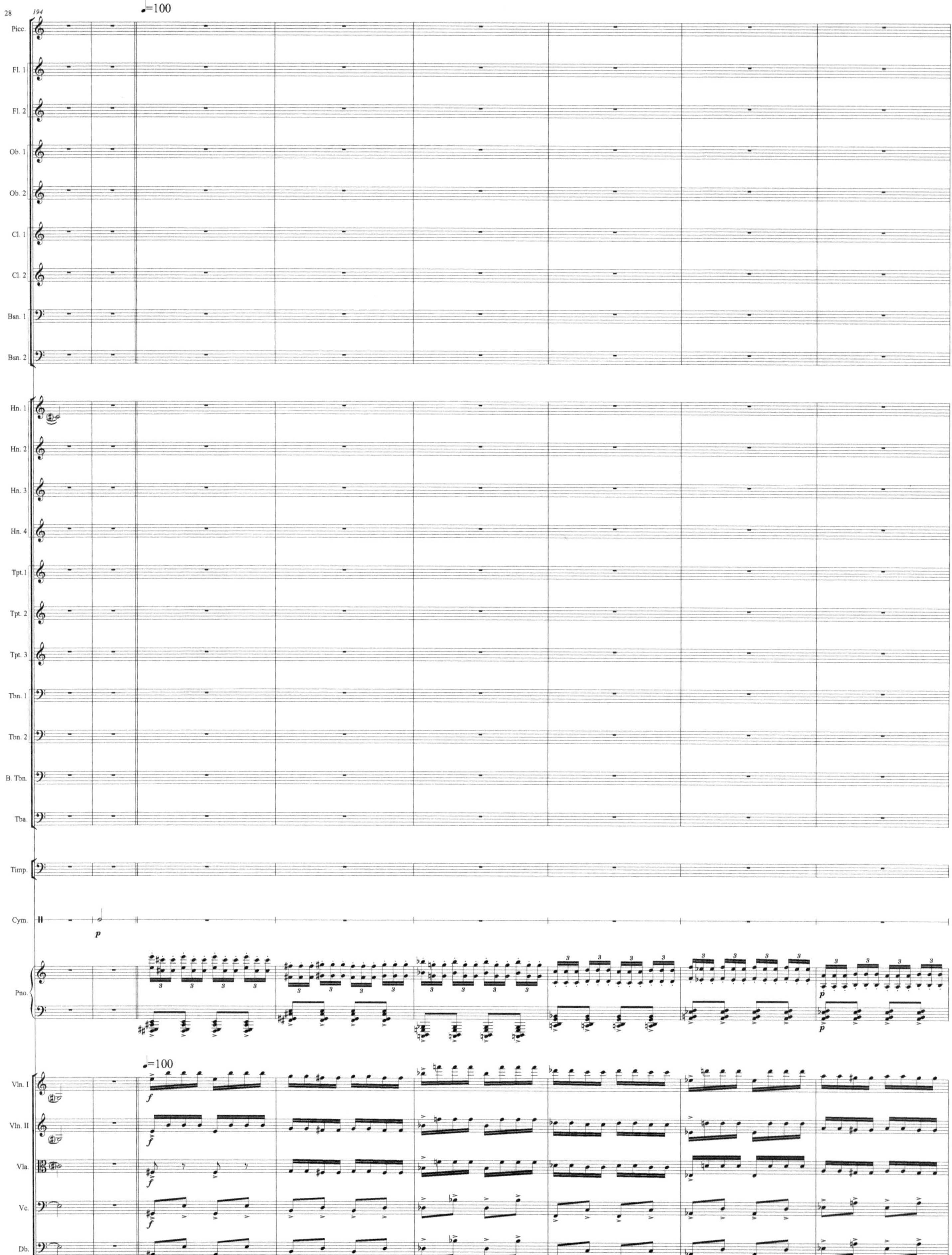
194
♩=100
Picc.
Fl. 1
Fl. 2
Ob. 1
Ob. 2
Cl. 1
Cl. 2
Bsn. 1
Bsn. 2
Hn. 1
Hn. 2
Hn. 3
Hn. 4
Tpt. 1
Tpt. 2
Tpt. 3
Tbn. 1
Tbn. 2
B. Tbn.
Tba.
Timp.
Cym.
p
Pno.
p
♩=100
Vln. I
f
Vln. II
f
Vla.
f
Vc.
f
Db.
f

202
Picc.
Fl. 1
Fl. 2
Ob. 1
Ob. 2
Cl. 1
Cl. 2
Bsn. 1
Bsn. 2
Hn. 1
Hn. 2
Hn. 3
Hn. 4
Tpt. 1
Tpt. 2
Tpt. 3
Tbn. 1
Tbn. 2
B. Tbn.
Tba.
Timp.
Cym.
Pno.
Vln. I
Vln. II
Vla.
Vc.
Db.
gliss.
div.
unis.

210
Picc.
Fl. 1
Fl. 2
Ob. 1
Ob. 2
Cl. 1
Cl. 2
Bsn. 1
Bsn. 2
Hn. 1
Hn. 2
Hn. 3
Hn. 4
Tpt. 1
Tpt. 2
Tpt. 3
Tbn. 1
Tbn. 2
B. Tbn.
Tba.
Timp.
Cym.
Pno.
Vln. I
Vln. II
Vla.
Vc.
Db.
gliss.
div.

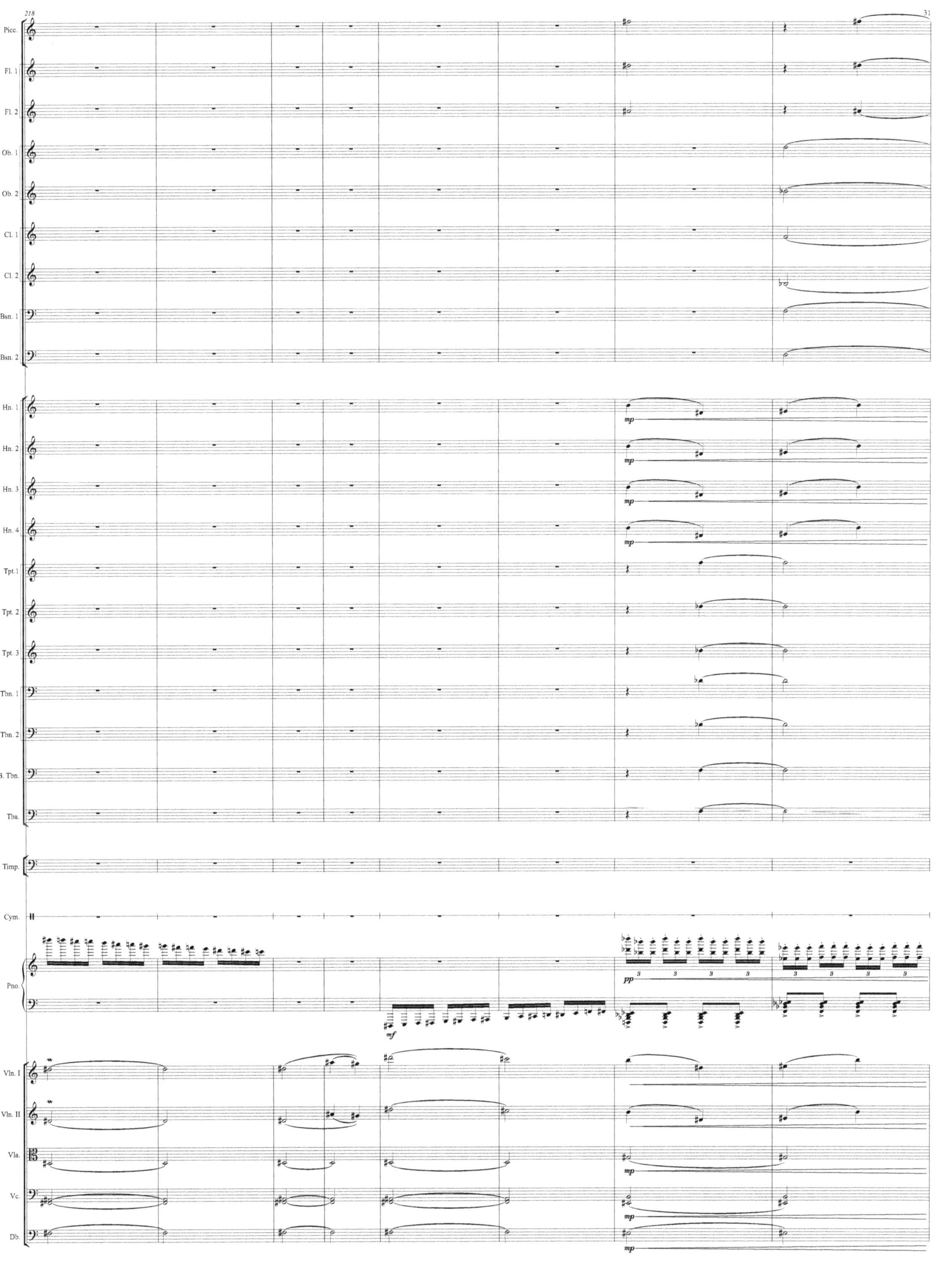
218
Picc.
Fl. 1
Fl. 2
Ob. 1
Ob. 2
Cl. 1
Cl. 2
Bsn. 1
Bsn. 2
Hn. 1
Hn. 2
Hn. 3
Hn. 4
Tpt. 1
Tpt. 2
Tpt. 3
Tbn. 1
Tbn. 2
B. Tbn.
Tba.
Timp.
Cym.
Pno.
Vln. I
Vln. II
Vla.
Vc.
Db.
mp
pp
mf

226
Picc.
Fl. 1
Fl. 2
Ob. 1
Ob. 2
Cl. 1
Cl. 2
Bsn. 1
Bsn. 2
Hn. 1
Hn. 2
Hn. 3
Hn. 4
Tpt. 1
Tpt. 2
Tpt. 3
Tbn. 1
Tbn. 2
B. Tbn.
Tba.
Timp.
Cym.
Pno.
Vln. I
Vln. II
Vla.
Vc.
Db.
gliss.
unis.

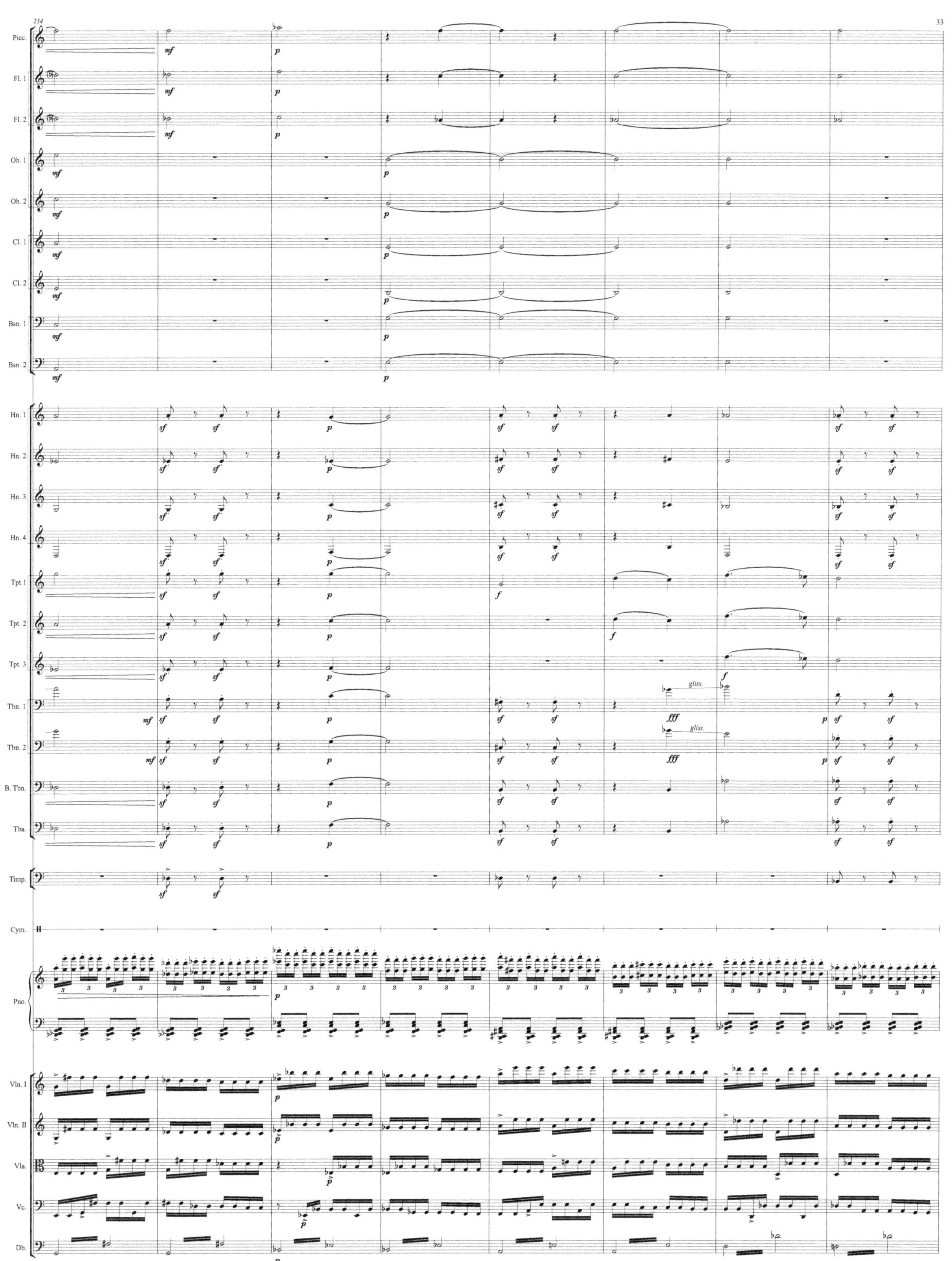
234
Picc.
Fl. 1
Fl. 2
Ob. 1
Ob. 2
Cl. 1
Cl. 2
Bsn. 1
Bsn. 2
Hn. 1
Hn. 2
Hn. 3
Hn. 4
Tpt.1
Tpt. 2
Tpt. 3
Tbn. 1
Tbn. 2
B. Tbn.
Tba.
Timp.
Cym.
Pno.
Vln. I
Vln. II
Vla.
Vc.
Db.
gliss.

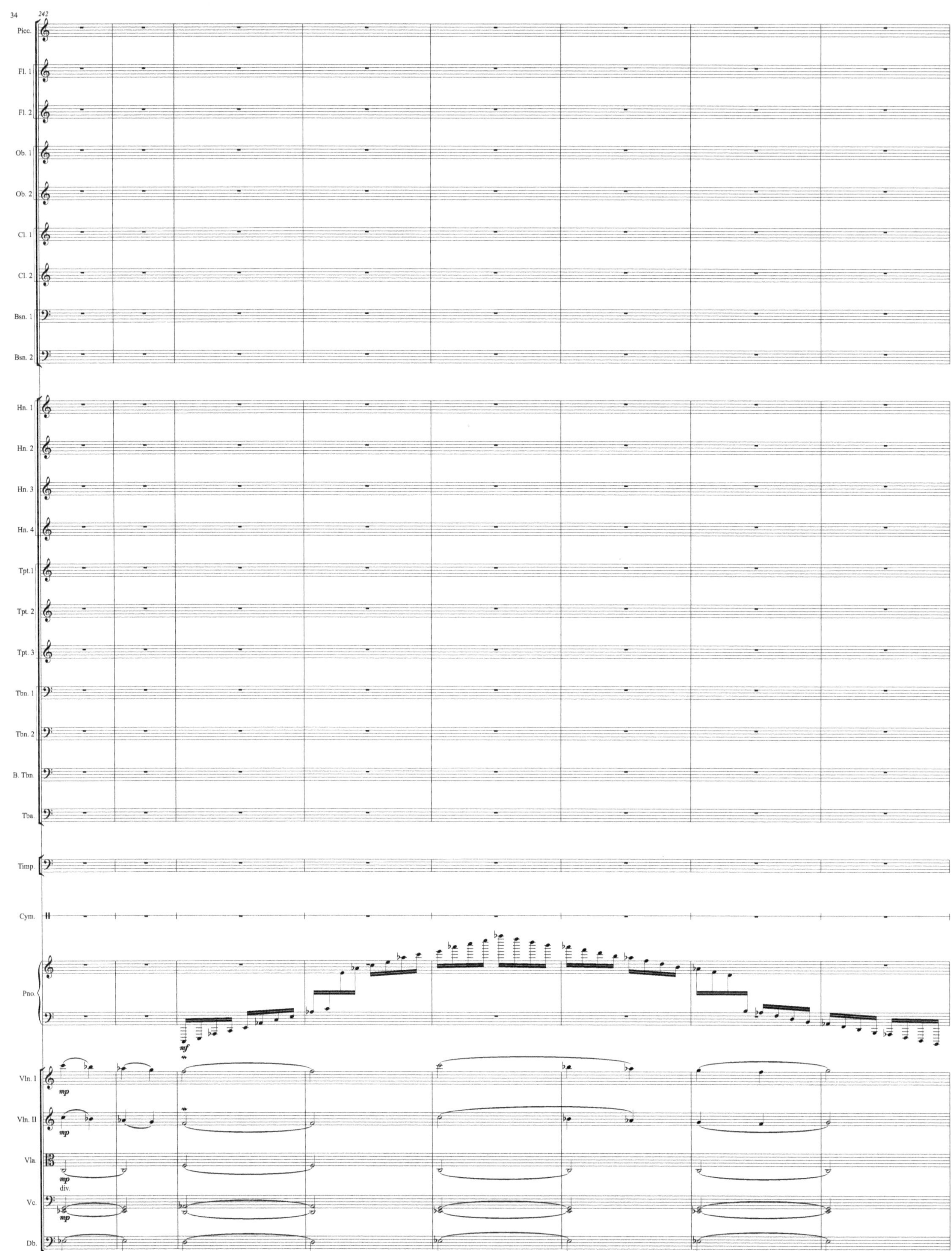
242
Picc.
Fl. 1
Fl. 2
Ob. 1
Ob. 2
Cl. 1
Cl. 2
Bsn. 1
Bsn. 2
Hn. 1
Hn. 2
Hn. 3
Hn. 4
Tpt. 1
Tpt. 2
Tpt. 3
Tbn. 1
Tbn. 2
B. Tbn.
Tba.
Timp.
Cym.
Pno.
mf
Vln. I
mp
Vln. II
mp
Vla.
mp
div.
Vc.
mp
Db.
mp

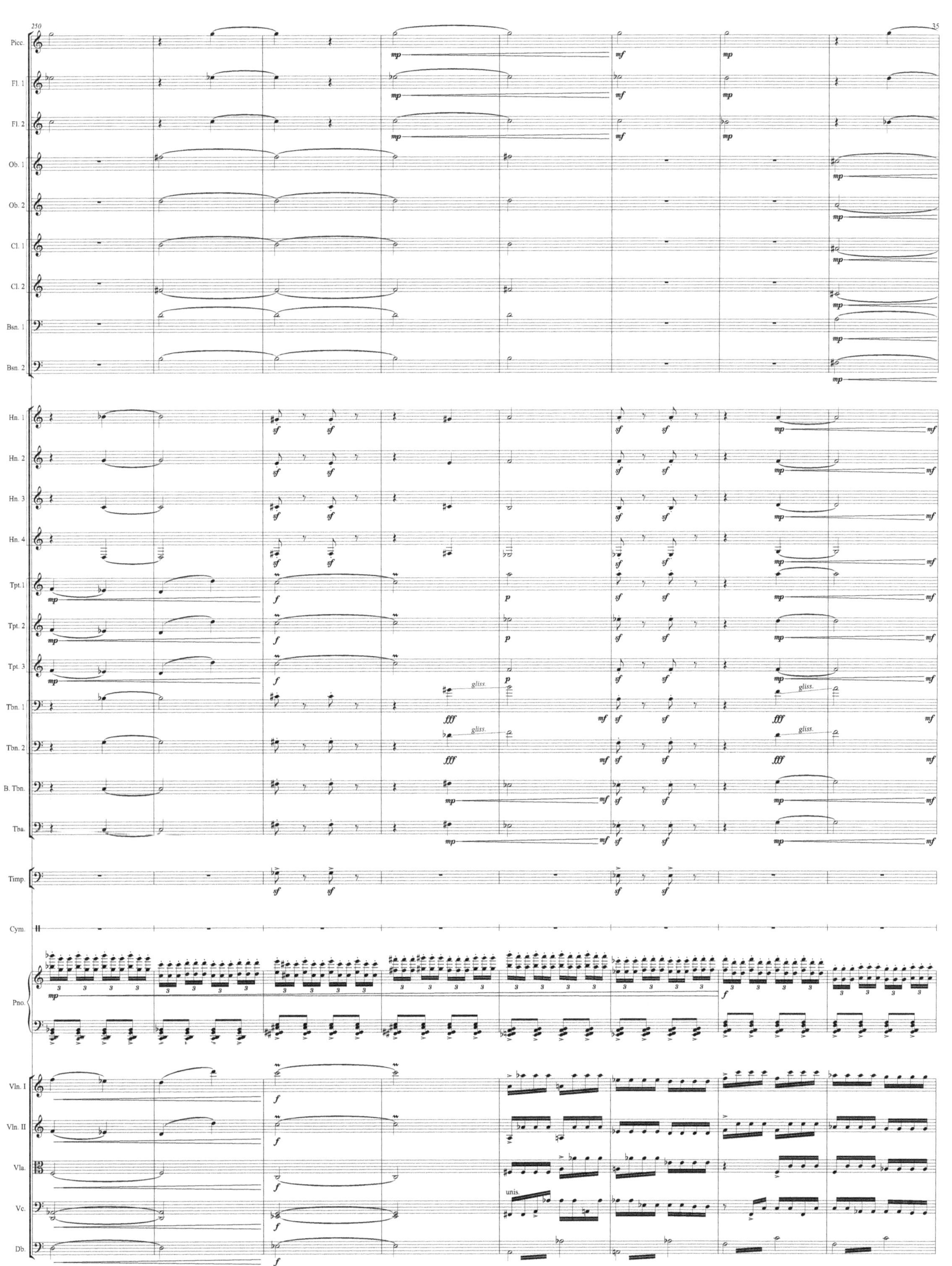
250
Picc.
Fl. 1
Fl. 2
Ob. 1
Ob. 2
Cl. 1
Cl. 2
Bsn. 1
Bsn. 2
Hn. 1
Hn. 2
Hn. 3
Hn. 4
Tpt. 1
Tpt. 2
Tpt. 3
Tbn. 1
Tbn. 2
B. Tbn.
Tba.
Timp.
Cym.
Pno.
Vln. I
Vln. II
Vla.
Vc.
Db.
gliss.
unis.

258
molto rit.
Picc.
Fl. 1
Fl. 2
Ob. 1
Ob. 2
Cl. 1
Cl. 2
Bsn. 1
Bsn. 2
Hn. 1
Hn. 2
Hn. 3
Hn. 4
Tpt. 1
Tpt. 2
Tpt. 3
Tbn. 1
Tbn. 2
B. Tbn.
Tba.
Timp.
Cym.
Pno.
Vln. I
Vln. II
Vla.
Vc.
Db.
gliss.
div.
molto rit.

266
♩=50
Picc.
Fl. 1
Fl. 2
Ob. 1
Ob. 2
Cl. 1
Cl. 2
Bsn. 1
Bsn. 2
Hn. 1
Hn. 2
Hn. 3
Hn. 4
Tpt. 1
Tpt. 2
Tpt. 3
Tbn. 1
Tbn. 2
B. Tbn.
Tba.
Timp.
Cym.
Pno.
Ped.
♩=50
div.
div.
Vln. I
Vln. II
Vla.
Vc.
Db.

274
Picc.
Fl. 1
Fl. 2
Ob. 1
Ob. 2
Cl. 1
Cl. 2
Bsn. 1
Bsn. 2
Hn. 1
Hn. 2
Hn. 3
Hn. 4
Tpt. 1
Tpt. 2
Tpt. 3
Tbn. 1
Tbn. 2
B. Tbn.
Tba.
Timp.
Cym.
Pno.
Vln. I
Vln. II
Vla.
Vc.
Db.
p
ppp
mp
pp

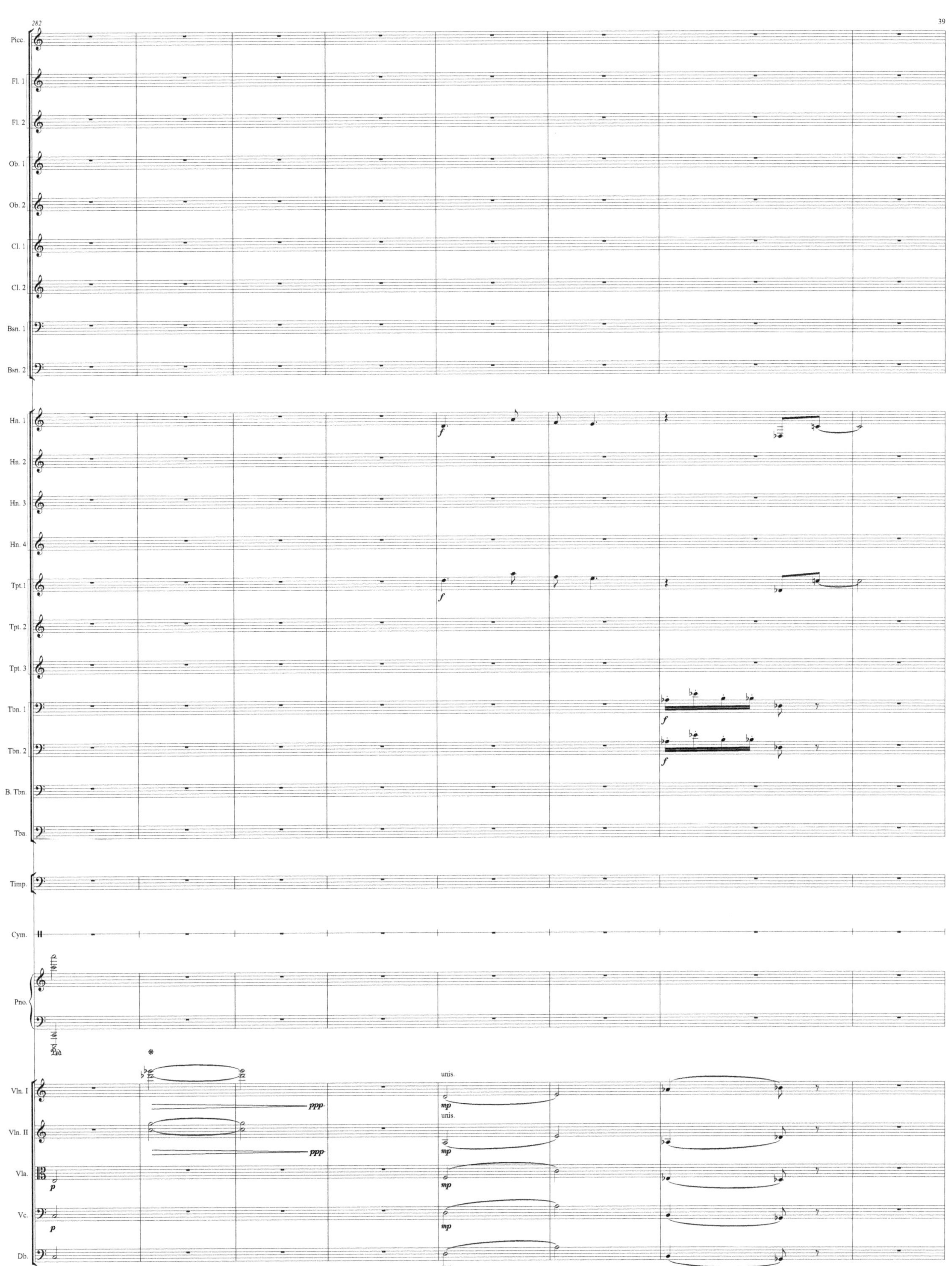
282
Picc.
Fl. 1
Fl. 2
Ob. 1
Ob. 2
Cl. 1
Cl. 2
Bsn. 1
Bsn. 2
Hn. 1
Hn. 2
Hn. 3
Hn. 4
Tpt. 1
Tpt. 2
Tpt. 3
Tbn. 1
Tbn. 2
B. Tbn.
Tba.
Timp.
Cym.
Pno.
Vln. I
Vln. II
Vla.
Vc.
Db.
unis.
f
mp
p
ppp

290
♩=80
Picc.
Fl. 1
Fl. 2
Ob. 1
Ob. 2
Cl. 1
Cl. 2
Bsn. 1
Bsn. 2
Hn. 1
Hn. 2
Hn. 3
Hn. 4
Tpt.1
Tpt. 2
Tpt. 3
Tbn. 1
Tbn. 2
B. Tbn.
Tba.
Timp.
Cym.
Pno.
♩=80
unis.
Vln. I
Vln. II
Vla.
Vc.
Db.

298
molto rall.
♩=80
molto accel.
Picc.
Fl. 1
Fl. 2
Ob. 1
Ob. 2
Cl. 1
Cl. 2
Bsn. 1
Bsn. 2
Hn. 1
Hn. 2
Hn. 3
Hn. 4
Tpt. 1
Tpt. 2
Tpt. 3
Tbn. 1
Tbn. 2
B. Tbn.
Tba.
Timp.
Cym.
Pno.
molto rall.
♩=80
molto accel.
Vln. I
Vln. II
Vla.
Vc.
Db.

306
Picc.
Fl. 1
Fl. 2
Ob. 1
Ob. 2
Cl. 1
Cl. 2
Bsn. 1
Bsn. 2
Hn. 1
Hn. 2
Hn. 3
Hn. 4
Tpt. 1
Tpt. 2
Tpt. 3
Tbn. 1
Tbn. 2
B. Tbn.
Tba.
Timp.
Cym.
Pno.
Vln. I
Vln. II
Vla.
Vc.
Db.
♩=80
fff
Ped.

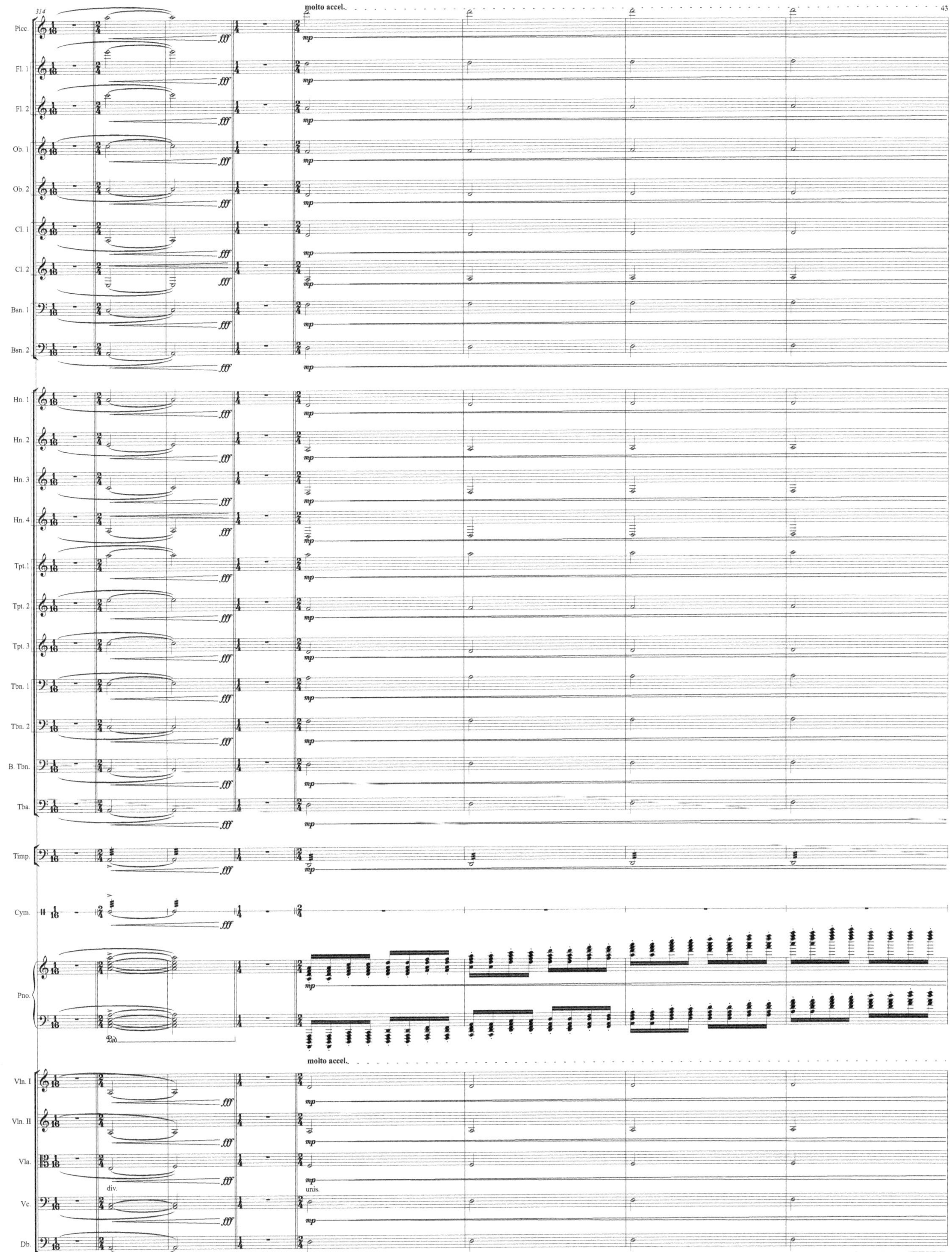
314
molto accel.
Picc.
Fl. 1
Fl. 2
Ob. 1
Ob. 2
Cl. 1
Cl. 2
Bsn. 1
Bsn. 2
Hn. 1
Hn. 2
Hn. 3
Hn. 4
Tpt. 1
Tpt. 2
Tpt. 3
Tbn. 1
Tbn. 2
B. Tbn.
Tba.
Timp.
Cym.
Pno.
Ped.
molto accel.
Vln. I
Vln. II
Vla.
div.
unis.
Vc.
Db.
fff
mp

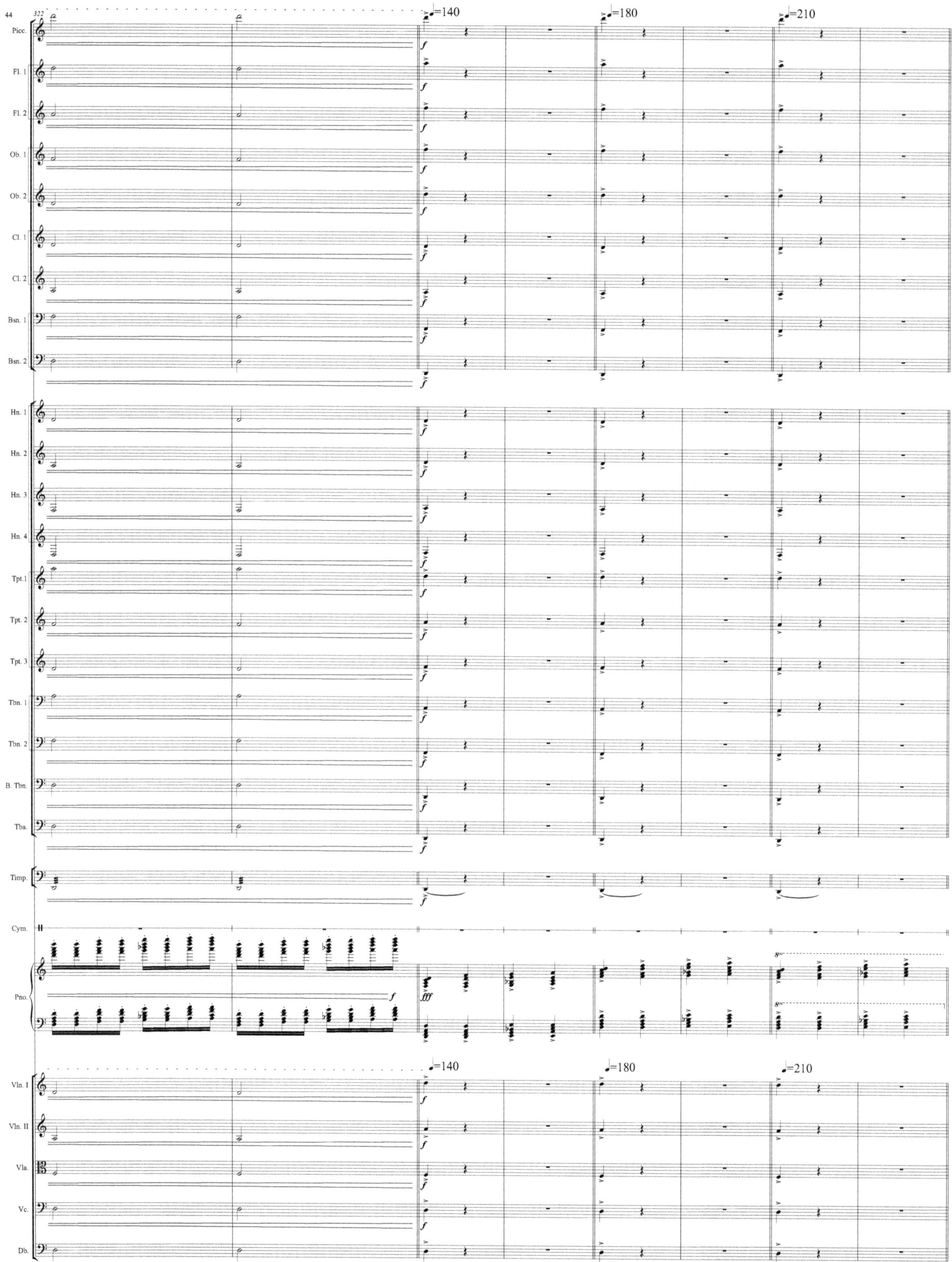
322
♩=140
♩=180
♩=210
Picc.
Fl. 1
Fl. 2
Ob. 1
Ob. 2
Cl. 1
Cl. 2
Bsn. 1
Bsn. 2
Hn. 1
Hn. 2
Hn. 3
Hn. 4
Tpt. 1
Tpt. 2
Tpt. 3
Tbn. 1
Tbn. 2
B. Tbn.
Tba.
Timp.
Cym.
Pno.
Vln. I
Vln. II
Vla.
Vc.
Db.

330
♩=240
♩=80
♩=50
Picc.
Fl. 1
Fl. 2
Ob. 1
Ob. 2
Cl. 1
Cl. 2
Bsn. 1
Bsn. 2
Hn. 1
Hn. 2
Hn. 3
Hn. 4
Tpt. 1
Tpt. 2
Tpt. 3
Tbn. 1
Tbn. 2
B. Tbn.
Tba.
Timp.
Cym.
gliss.
31
7
p
f
Pno.
Vln. I
Vln. II
Vla.
Vc.
Db.

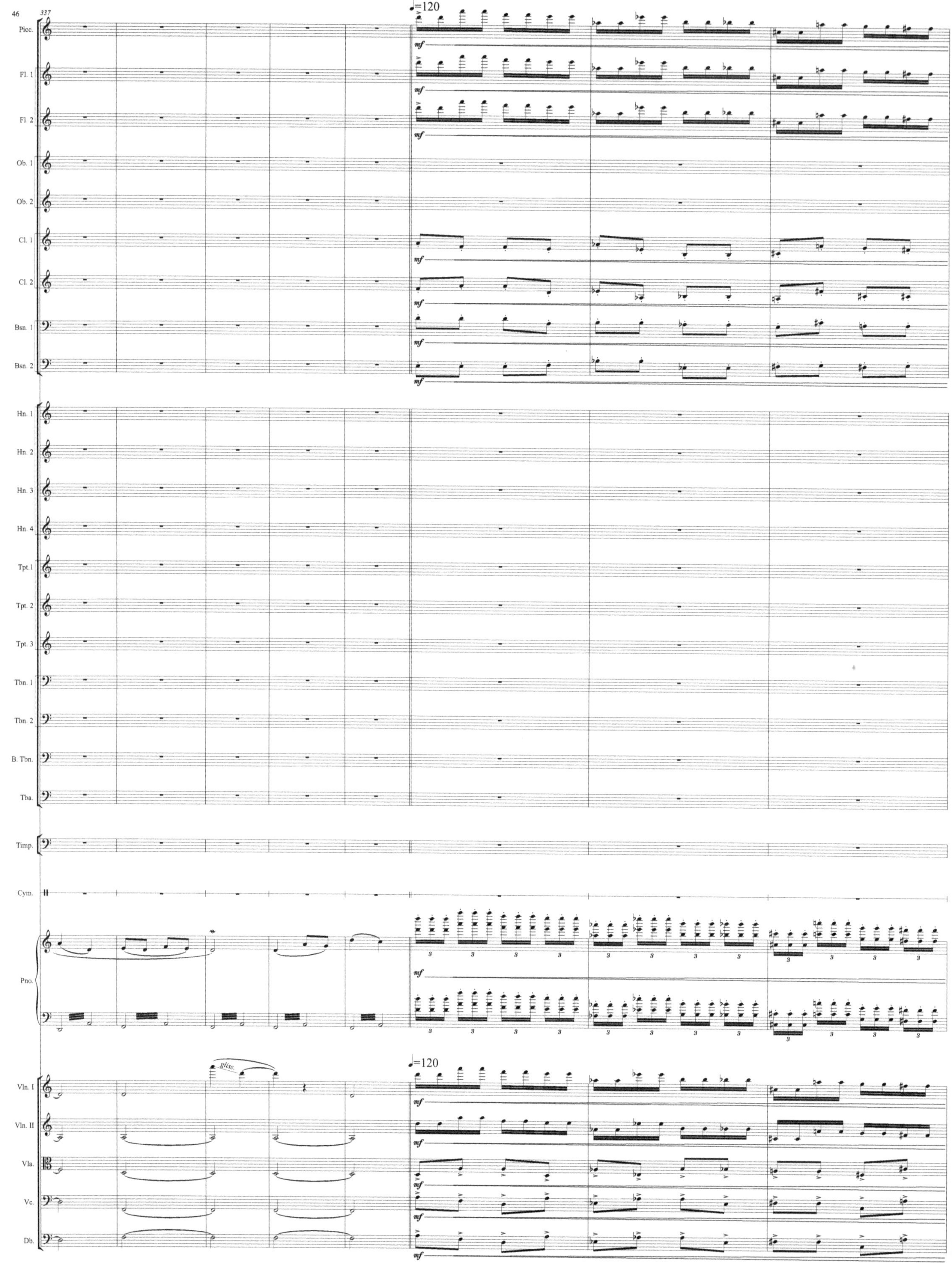
337
♩=120
Picc.
Fl. 1
Fl. 2
Ob. 1
Ob. 2
Cl. 1
Cl. 2
Bsn. 1
Bsn. 2
Hn. 1
Hn. 2
Hn. 3
Hn. 4
Tpt. 1
Tpt. 2
Tpt. 3
Tbn. 1
Tbn. 2
B. Tbn.
Tba.
Timp.
Cym.
Pno.
gliss.
♩=120
Vln. I
Vln. II
Vla.
Vc.
Db.

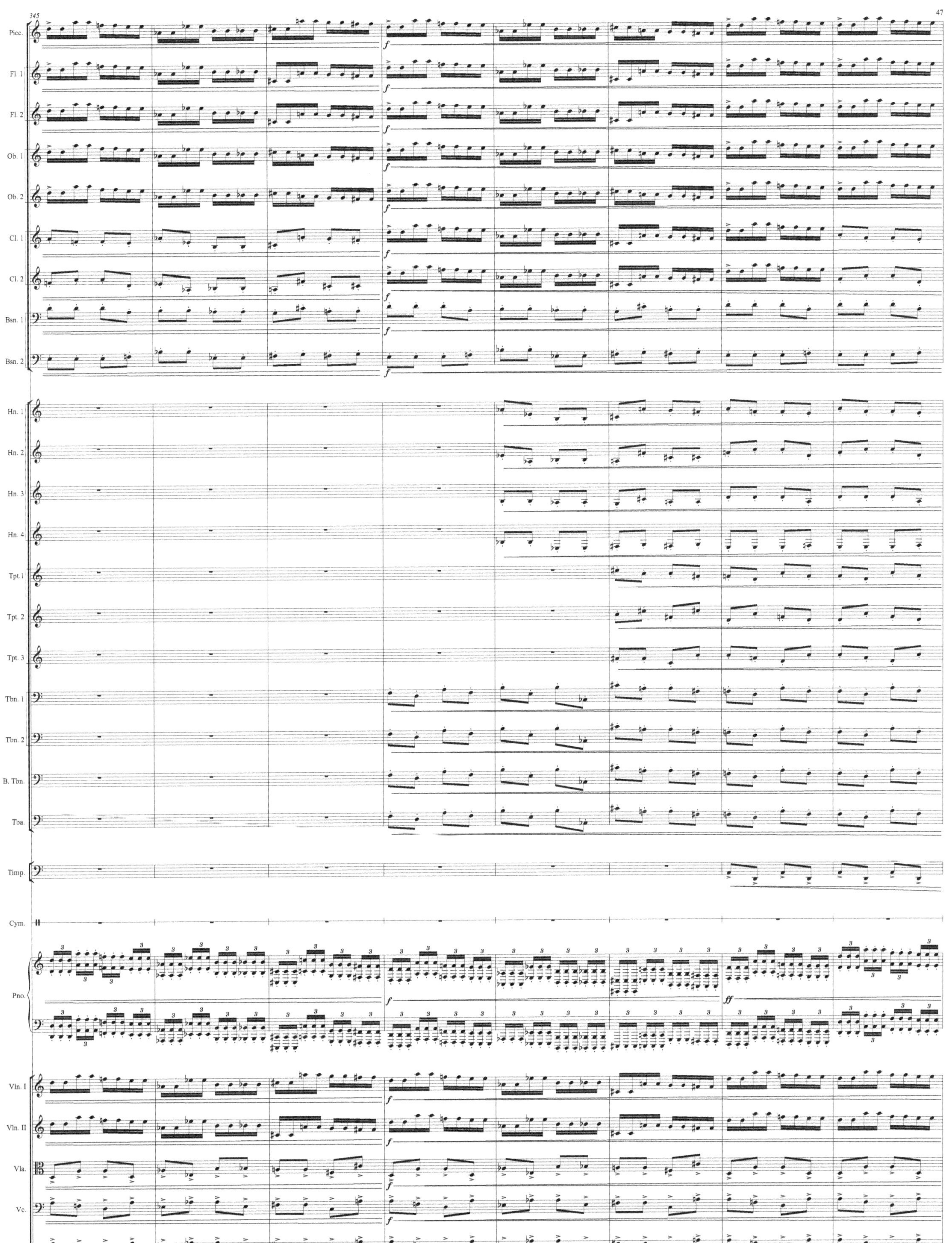
345
Picc.
Fl. 1
Fl. 2
Ob. 1
Ob. 2
Cl. 1
Cl. 2
Bsn. 1
Bsn. 2
Hn. 1
Hn. 2
Hn. 3
Hn. 4
Tpt. 1
Tpt. 2
Tpt. 3
Tbn. 1
Tbn. 2
B. Tbn.
Tba.
Timp.
Cym.
Pno.
Vln. I
Vln. II
Vla.
Vc.
Db.

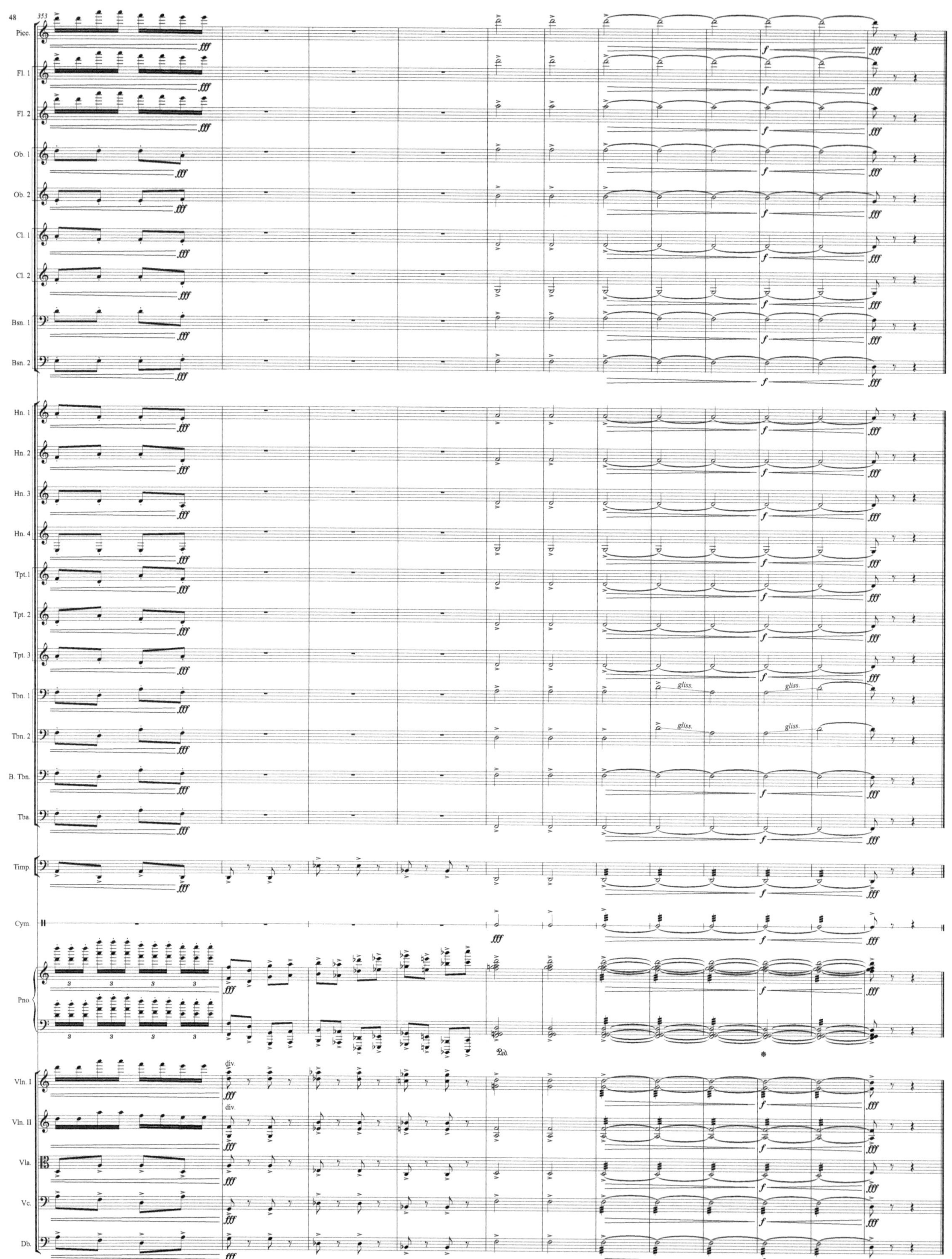
353
Picc.
Fl. 1
Fl. 2
Ob. 1
Ob. 2
Cl. 1
Cl. 2
Bsn. 1
Bsn. 2
Hn. 1
Hn. 2
Hn. 3
Hn. 4
Tpt. 1
Tpt. 2
Tpt. 3
Tbn. 1
Tbn. 2
B. Tbn.
Tba.
Timp.
Cym.
Pno.
Vln. I
Vln. II
Vla.
Vc.
Db.
fff
f
gliss.
div.
Ped.

www.ingramcontent.com/pod-product-compliance
Lightning Source LLC
Chambersburg PA
CBHW081141090426
42736CB00018B/3444
9780578723020